KT-594-736

SHAPES

CIRCLES
CYLINDERS & SPHERES

PETER PATILLA

BELITHA PRESS

First published in Great Britain in 1994 by

Belitha Press Limited

31 Newington Green, London N16 9PU

Text copyright © Peter Patilla 1994

Format and illustrations copyright © Belitha Press Ltd 1994

All rights reserved. No part of this book may be reproduced or utilized in any form or by any means, electronic or mechanical, including photocopying, recording or by any information storage and retrieval system, without permission in writing from the Publisher.

Printed in Hong Kong for Imago

ISBN 1 85561 274 7 (hardback)

ISBN 1 85561 331 X (paperback)

British Library Cataloguing in Publication Data CIP data for this book is available from the British Library

Acknowledgements

Photographic credits: J. Allan Cash: pages 6 (centre left), 19 (top right), 20 (bottom left), 21 (top right), 23 (top right); Ancient Art and Architecture Collection: page 18 (top centre); Robert Harding Picture Library: pages 6 (bottom), 7 (bottom left), 14 (top right), 18 (bottom), 20 (bottom right), 22 (bottom), 24 (bottom right); Hulton-Deutsch Collection: page 23 (top left); Image Bank, London: pages 16 (top left), 21 (bottom right); Tony Stone Worldwide: pages 11 (bottom right), 25 (bottom), 26 (bottom left), 27 (top right), 29 (bottom).

All other photographs by Claire Paxton

Illustrations: Jonathan Satchell

Mobile and string curves: Deborah Crow

Editor: Rachel Cooke

Designer: John Calvert

Picture researcher: Juliet Duff

Thanks to our models Sally and Dapo

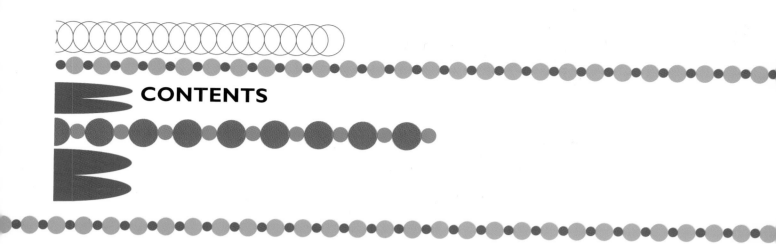

CONTENTS

WHAT IS A CIRCLE?

A circle is a round, two-dimensional shape with a centre and a **circumference.** Each point on the circumference of a circle is the same distance from the centre. The circumference of a circle is sometimes called its perimeter.

The word circle comes from the Latin word *circulus*. Other words to do with roundness also begin with *circ* – think of circus, circuit and circulate.

All these shapes are circles.

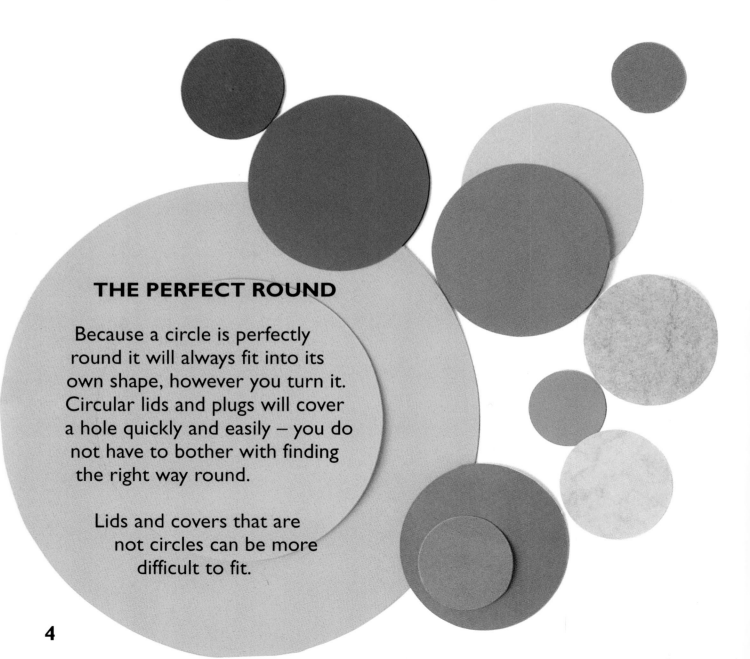

THE PERFECT ROUND

Because a circle is perfectly round it will always fit into its own shape, however you turn it. Circular lids and plugs will cover a hole quickly and easily – you do not have to bother with finding the right way round.

Lids and covers that are not circles can be more difficult to fit.

CIRCLES EVERYWHERE

Sometimes shapes are very nearly circles. The circumference may not be quite a smooth line. Because these shapes are very nearly circles, we can call them circular shapes. Circular shapes can be found all around us.

CIRCLES IN CIRCLES

Sometimes different sized circles radiate out from the same centre. When this happens they are called **concentric circles**.

Concentric circles are used on archery targets.

These concentric circles will tell us the age of the tree. Every year a new circle is added.

When a concentric circle is cut from a larger concentric circle, the shape which remains is called an **annulus.** An annulus looks rather like a washer.

Drop something into the water and see the concentric circles.

SPINNING AND TURNING

Some circles are like wheels. The centre of the circle has an axle or pivot – this allows the circle to turn or spin.

Things which spin around a centre make a circle shape.

INTERLOCKING TEETH

Some circles or wheels have teeth around their circumference – they are called cogs. The teeth fit into each other and once one cog turns so do all the others.

SUPER SPINNER

You can make your own spinning circle.

1. Draw round a mug with a circular base onto some card and cut out the circle. Draw patterns on both sides.

2. Make two holes, about 1 cm apart on either side of the centre.

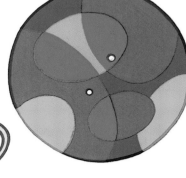

3. Cut a piece of thin string about 150 cm long and thread it through each of the holes. Knot the two ends together to make a loop.

4. Hold the loop with both hands with the card circle in the middle. By gently tugging and relaxing on the string, the circle will begin to spin.
What happens to the patterns on the card?

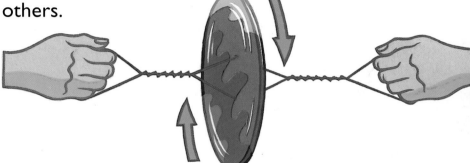

DRAWING CIRCLES

The easiest way to draw a circle is to draw around circular objects. Drawing circles freehand is more difficult. It is even harder than drawing straight lines.

String can also be helpful when drawing circles, especially large ones.

The picture shows you how.

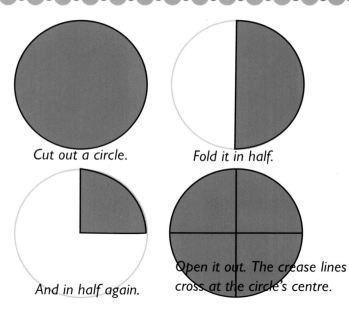

Cut out a circle.

Fold it in half.

And in half again.

Open it out. The crease lines cross at the circle's centre.

FINDING THE CENTRE

Once you've drawn a circle, cut it out. Fold the circle in half, then in half again. Open out the circle. The circle's centre is where the creases cross.

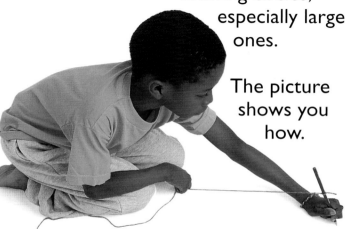

A pin or your finger provides the centre point, while the pencil draws the circumference. By keeping the string taut, you make sure the pencil is always exactly the same distance from the centre.

Here are two kinds of instruments which can be used to draw circles.

CIRCULAR PATTERNS

You can make interesting designs and patterns using circles. Compasses and a sharp pencil are the best tools for this.

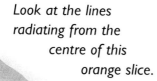

Follow these drawings to make a circular flower. See what other patterns you can create.

Look at the lines radiating from the centre of this orange slice.

LINES INSIDE CIRCLES

You can draw several different straight lines inside a circle. They all have special names.

FROM THE CENTRE
Any straight line which goes from the centre to the circumference is called a **radius.** *More than one radius are called radii. The word radius is a Latin word meaning rod or spoke. The spokes on some wheels are radii.*

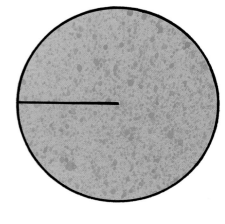

THROUGH THE CENTRE
Any straight line which goes across a circle, through the centre, is called a **diameter**. *The word diameter comes from a Greek word meaning through or across. A diameter is the same length as two radii.*

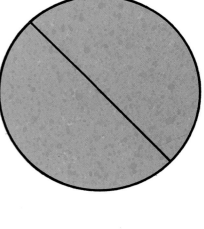

JOINING THE CIRCUMFERENCE
Any straight line which goes across a circle, but not through the centre, is called a **chord**. *The word chord comes from a Greek word meaning a string.*

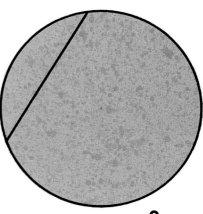

PARTS OF A CIRCLE

Circles are often divided into different parts. Half a circle is called a **semicircle**. Quarter of a circle is called a **quadrant**.

Semicircle

Quadrant

CUT FROM THE CENTRE

A wedge cut from a circle with two radii as edges divides the circle into two **sectors**. The smaller slice is called the **minor sector** and the larger is called the **major sector**. The word sector comes from a Latin word meaning to cut.

Japanese fans are like sectors of a circle.

Pizzas are often cut into sectors. Can you think of any other food which is also cut into sectors?

You can make your own fan by folding up a piece of paper into small zig-zags. Fasten one end of the folded paper with an elastic band or staple. See if you can join some fans together to make a circular shape.

A clock's pendulum swings in an arc

CUT FROM THE SIDE

A slice cut along a chord of a circle divides it into two **segments**. The smaller piece is called the **minor segment** and the larger is the **major segment**. The word segment comes from a Latin word meaning to cut off.

PART OF THE EDGE

Part of a circumference is called an **arc**. An arc which is smaller than a semicircle is called a **minor arc** and one which is larger than a semicircle is called a **major arc**. The word arc comes from a Latin word meaning bow.

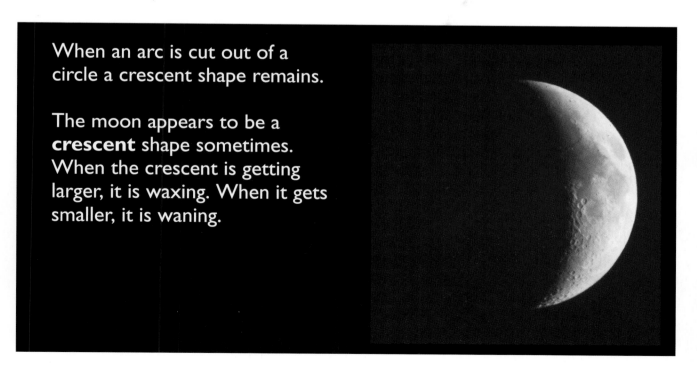

When an arc is cut out of a circle a crescent shape remains.

The moon appears to be a **crescent** shape sometimes. When the crescent is getting larger, it is waxing. When it gets smaller, it is waning.

OVALS

An **oval** is another sort of 2-D shape with no straight edges. The word oval comes from a Latin word meaning egg.

Oval describes two sorts of shape. One is an egg shape, where one end is more pointed than the other. The second shape is like a slightly flattened circle. This kind of oval is also called an **ellipse**. When you look at a circle from an angle, it looks like an ellipse.

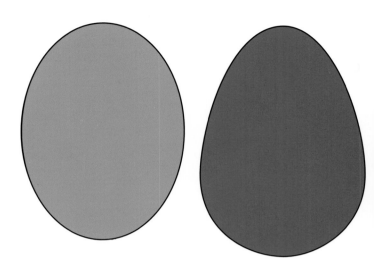

DIVIDING AN OVAL

An egg shape oval can be folded in half only. But an ellipse can be folded in half then into quarters.

Fold a sheet of paper into quarters and draw an arc around the corner of the fold. Cut along the arc and open out the shape. Is it an ellipse? Try making a circle in this way.

From this angle these circular tops look like ellipses.

THE MAGIC EGG

This is an old puzzle based on the problem posed by the question: which came first: the chicken or the egg? An oval is divided into nine pieces. The pieces can be arranged to make bird pictures.

You can make your own magic egg by tracing the outlines of the shapes in the oval shown here onto thin card. Cut along the lines and see if you can make some bird shapes from the pieces.

CURVES

A **curve** is a line which has no straight part. Curves are all around us.

Spirals are a special type of curve.

OPEN OR CLOSED

An open curve has two ends. An arc is an open curve.
A closed curve has no ends. Circles and ovals are both closed curves.

Mazes were often made from circular designs with lots of interesting curves inside them.
Look for the curves in these puzzle mazes.

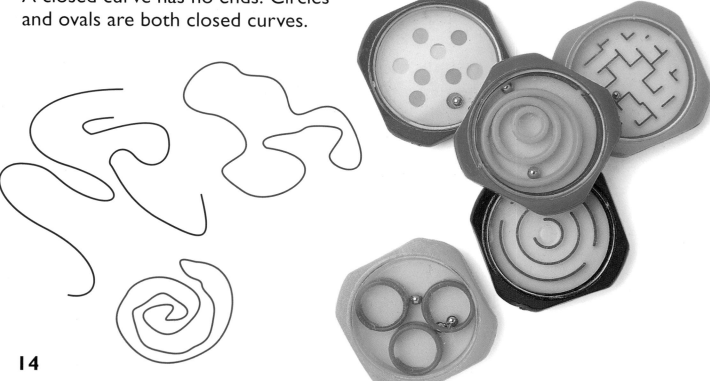

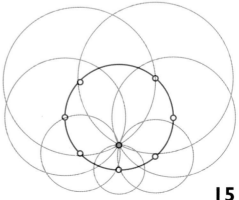

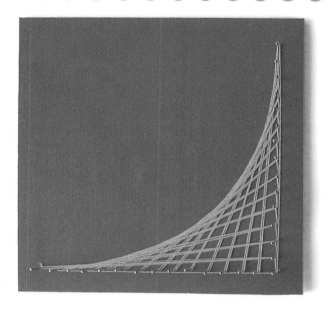

STRAIGHT TO CURVED

Straight lines can be positioned in such a way that they appear to make arcs, circles and curves. The more lines that are drawn the smoother the curve.

Try making a curve from straight lines like this:

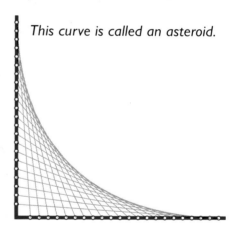

This curve is called an asteroid.

CURVED PATTERNS

1. Draw a circle and put some dots around the circumference. Put one dot just inside the circle.

2. Put a compass point on one of the circumference dots and draw a circle whose circumference passes through the inside dot.

3. Repeat step two for every dot on the circumference of your original circle.

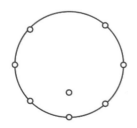

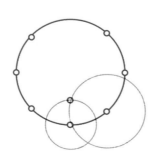

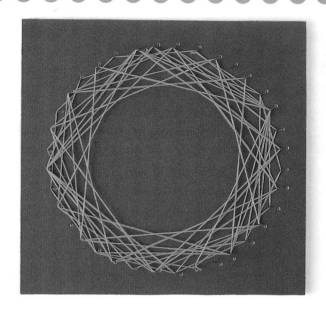

RINGS AND LOOPS

Curves can form part of shapes that are three-dimensional (3-D). This means the shape is not flat but has height as well as length and width. One 3-D shape formed from a curve is a **torus**. This is like an anchor ring – such as a doughnut or inner-tube. A torus has no flat surfaces.

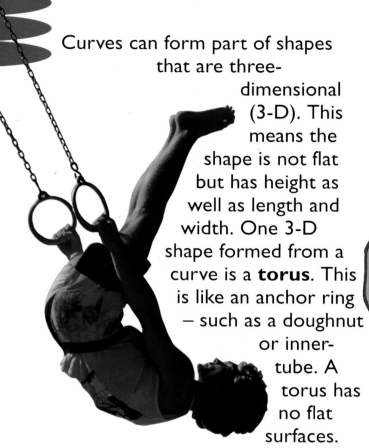

Rings can go round shirts and socks.

Jewellery can come in rings and loops.

A doughnut ring is shaped like a torus.

The word ring is sometimes used to describe a loop or anything which is a circular shape.

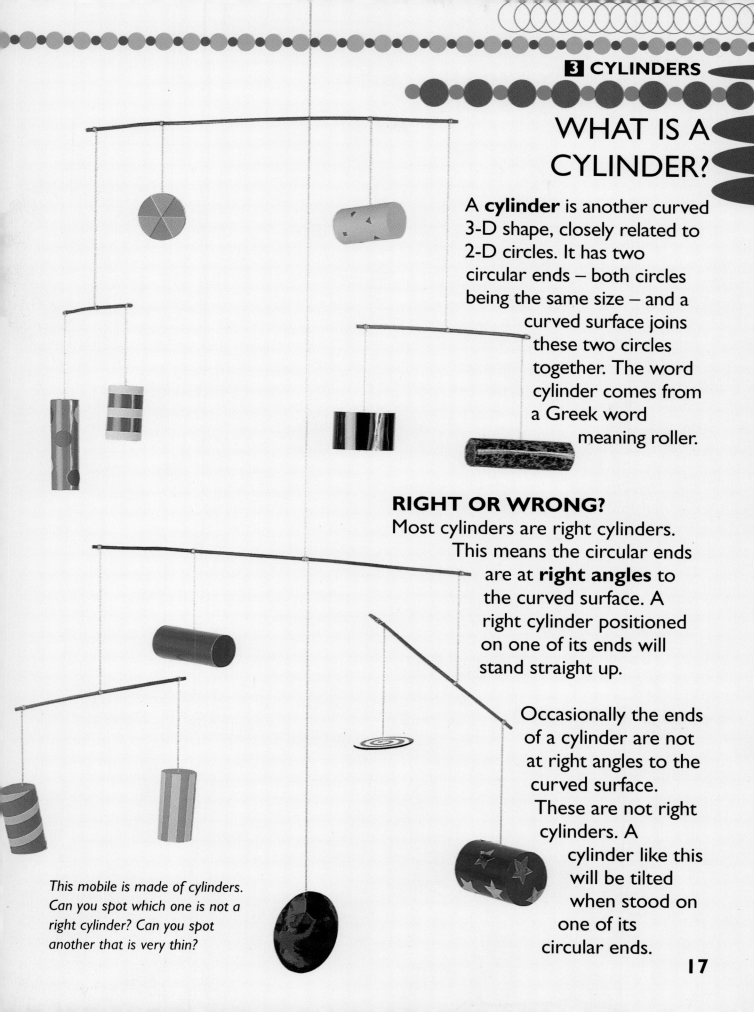

WHAT IS A CYLINDER?

A **cylinder** is another curved 3-D shape, closely related to 2-D circles. It has two circular ends – both circles being the same size – and a curved surface joins these two circles together. The word cylinder comes from a Greek word meaning roller.

RIGHT OR WRONG?

Most cylinders are right cylinders. This means the circular ends are at **right angles** to the curved surface. A right cylinder positioned on one of its ends will stand straight up.

Occasionally the ends of a cylinder are not at right angles to the curved surface. These are not right cylinders. A cylinder like this will be tilted when stood on one of its circular ends.

This mobile is made of cylinders. Can you spot which one is not a right cylinder? Can you spot another that is very thin?

CYLINDERS EVERYWHERE

You can spot cylinders almost everywhere you look.

STORAGE SPACE
Cylinders can be hollow and then filled with all sorts of interesting things. Cylinders are the most common shape of tin you will find on supermarket shelves.

Very thin cylinders, like coins, are often called **discs** (sometimes spelt disks). The word disc comes from a Greek word discus. Throwing the discus was a popular sport in ancient Greece and is still an event in athletics today.

CYLINDER SUPPORTS

The cylinder is quite a strong shape which is why it is often used in building as columns to hold roofs up.

Columns are often made to look attractive through using fancy tops and bottoms.

The famous Parthenon columns in Greece are stone cylinders.

MOVING WITH CYLINDERS

Since the earliest times, humans have used cylinders to help them move things. The cylinders acted as rollers. Eventually rollers became wheels with axles.

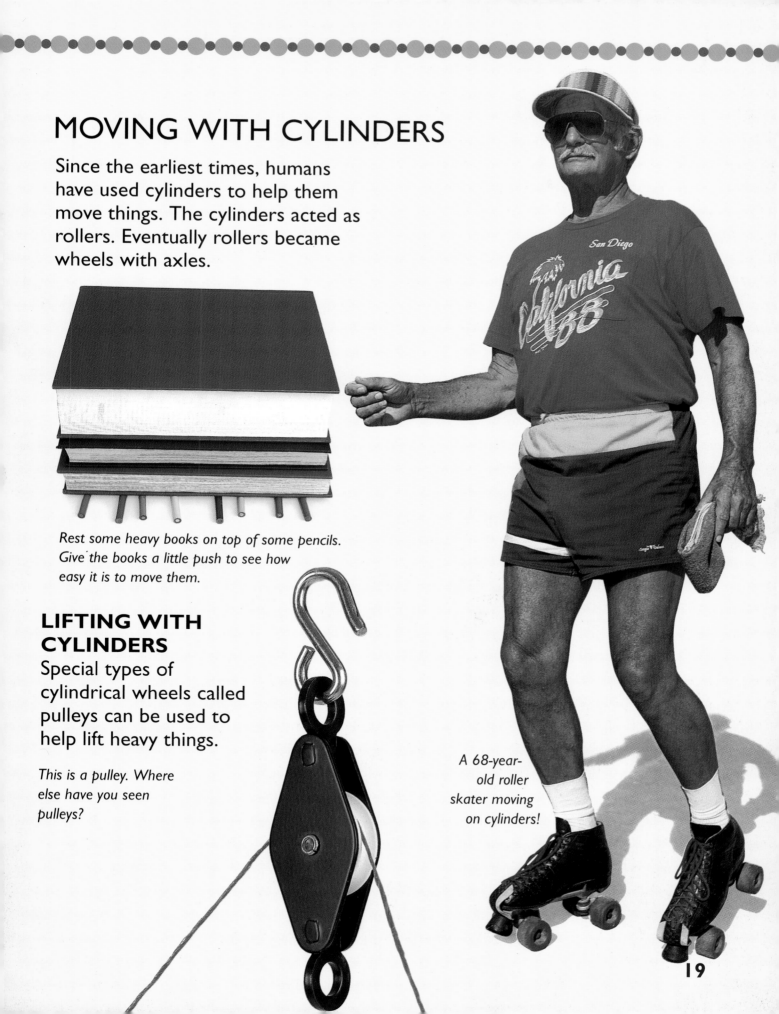

Rest some heavy books on top of some pencils. Give the books a little push to see how easy it is to move them.

LIFTING WITH CYLINDERS

Special types of cylindrical wheels called pulleys can be used to help lift heavy things.

This is a pulley. Where else have you seen pulleys?

A 68-year-old roller skater moving on cylinders!

TUBES AND PIPES

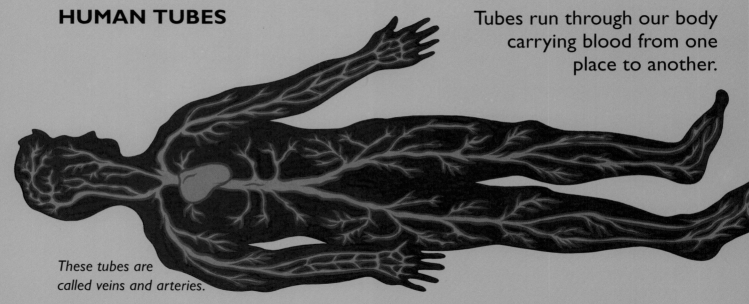

Hollow cylinders without solid ends become tubes and pipes.

Tubes and pipes are very useful. They can be used for sucking up liquids.

HUMAN TUBES

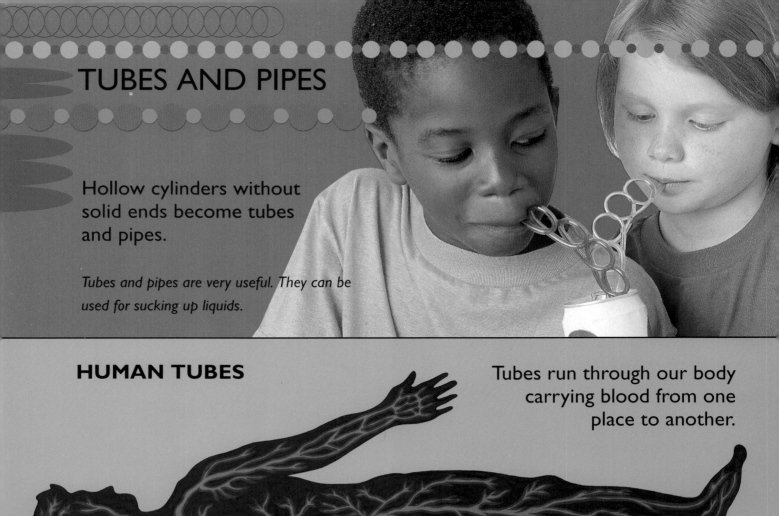

Tubes run through our body carrying blood from one place to another.

These tubes are called veins and arteries.

MUSICAL TUBES
Many musical instruments use tubes and cylinders.

A cylindrical 'Duala' drum.

Some tubes bend and change in size.

WHICH IS STRONGER?

Hollow tubes are very strong which is why they are used for scaffolding when building.
You can see a tube's strength for yourself by doing the following test.

You will need: 2 pieces of paper (about 20 x 30 cm), sticky tape, two thick books, a yoghurt pot and some small weights (pebbles will do).

1. Roll up one piece of paper very tightly to make a solid cylindrical rod. Fasten it with sticky tape.

2. Roll the other piece of paper around a pencil to make a tube. Fasten this with tape and remove the pencil.

3. Put the two books about 14 cm apart and place the rod and the tube across the gap between them. They should be about 5 cm apart.

4. Balance the yoghurt pot on the rod and the tube. Put weights into the pot until one of the paper supports begins to bend. You can probably guess which bends first!

Scaffolding tubes around the statue of Liberty.

Tunnels are quite like tubes laid on their sides.

SPECIAL CYLINDERS

Try making your own helix coded message with a pencil and a long thin strip of paper.

Cylinders have been adapted by people for special uses.
Water wheels or paddle wheels are special cylinders.
Large stone cylinders are used to grind cereals and to sharpen tools.

String wrapped round a cylinder makes a spiral shape called a helix. In fact, helix comes from a Greek word meaning spiral. We can see the helix spiral in all sorts of places.

The thread on each screw is a helix.

A CYLINDRICAL SECRET

The Greeks used the helix to write secret codes to each other. A messenger's belt would be wrapped round a cylinder in a spiral shape. The message was then written along the spiral with some other random letters and words to make it a code. When the belt was unwound from the cylinder, the message looked like a jumble of letters. Unless you knew the right size of cylinder to use the message could not be read.

A paddle-steamer on the Mississippi River.

NATCHEZ.

HOOPS

A hoop is usually a narrow hollow cylinder without ends.

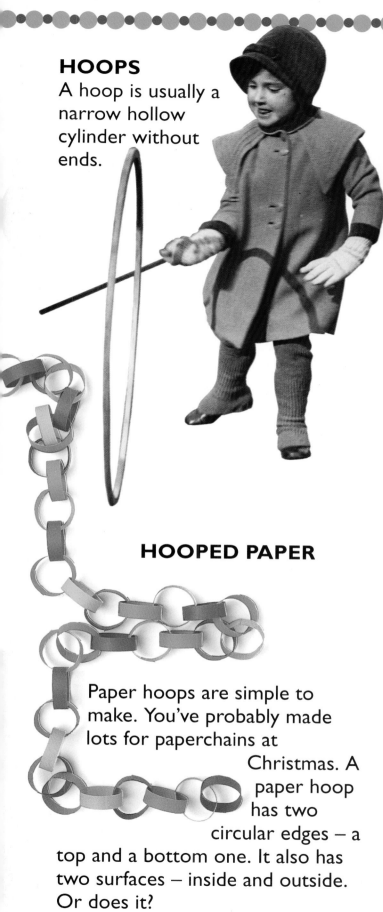

(above) Hoops were used to hold the parts of a wooden barrel together.
(left) Many years ago children used to roll hoops along the ground. They would run in and out of the hoop as it rolled along, trying not to touch it.

August Möbius, a German mathematician, invented a special kind of hoop with a twist in it. The twist only turns through a semicircle. Make one out of paper like the one below

HOOPED PAPER

Paper hoops are simple to make. You've probably made lots for paperchains at Christmas. A paper hoop has two circular edges – a top and a bottom one. It also has two surfaces – inside and outside. Or does it?

Run your finger around the edge of the hoop. You will find that your finger seems to travel along both the top and the bottom of the hoop – there is only one edge!

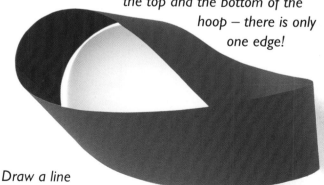

Draw a line along the middle of the hoop. By the time you get back to where you started, the line will appear to be on the inside and outside of the hoop – there is only one surface!

23

WHAT IS A SPHERE?

A **sphere** is a perfectly round ball. The distance from the centre of the sphere to anywhere on its surface is always the same.

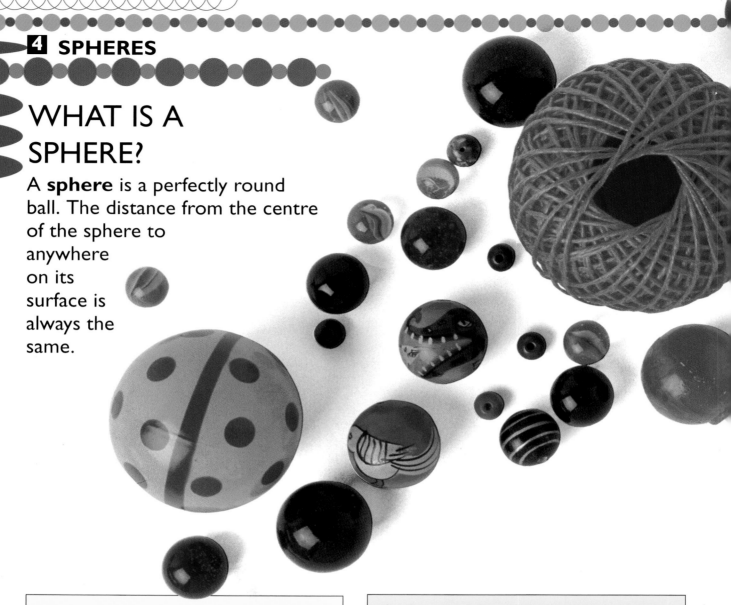

A SPINNING CIRCLE

Spin a coin on a table top and you will see a sphere shape. A circle spinning around its diameter makes a sphere.

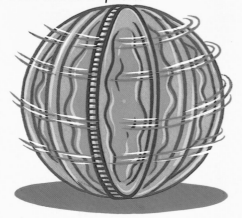

A sphere can be solid or hollow. It is very strong and can stand powerful forces pressing in on it.

24

ALL KINDS OF SPHERES

There are many kinds of spheres, made both by nature and by people. Some shapes are very nearly spheres. We call them spherical. There are a few on this page. See how many more you can spot around you.

Bubble gum can be blown into a spherical shape. The largest bubble gum bubble ever blown had a diameter of 55.8 cm. It was blown by Susan Montgomery in California.

Even some buildings use spheres. This is the Atomium in Brussels.

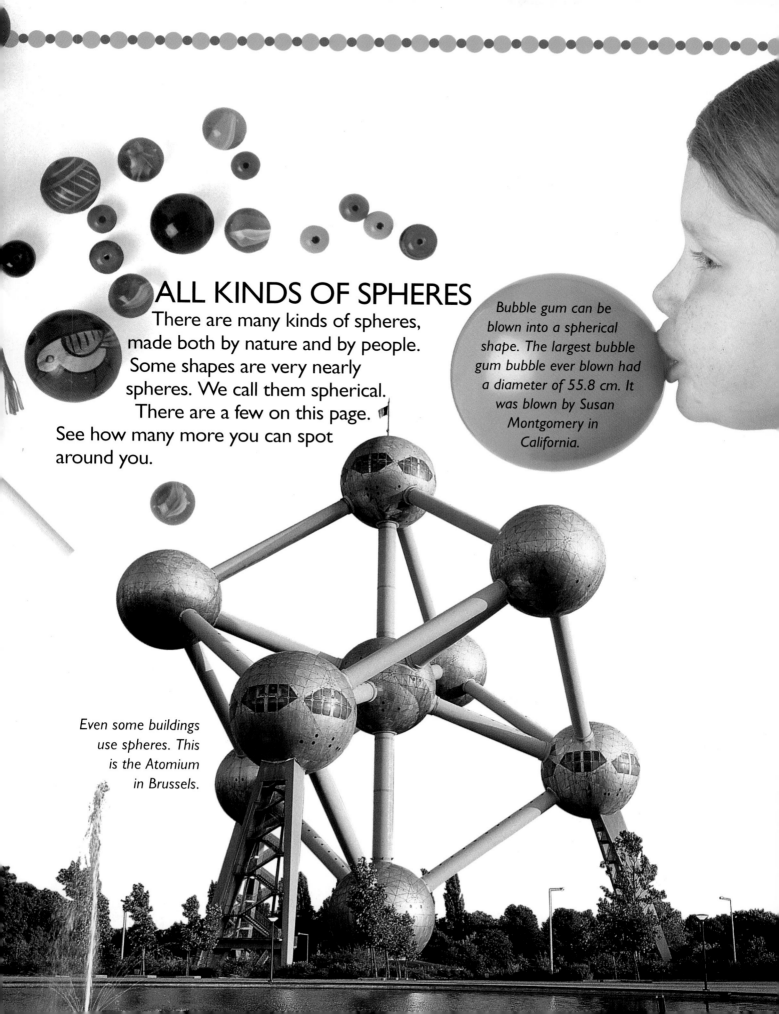

GAMES WITH SPHERES

The shape of a sphere makes it ideal for rolling smoothly in all directions. They are also good for catching and bouncing. Because of this, many games involve moving spherical balls. The skill comes in controlling the direction the balls move in.

Controlling balls by kicking and throwing.

PARTS OF A SPHERE

Like circles, spheres can be divided into parts. Half a sphere is called a **hemisphere.**

Can you spot the shapes that could form part of a sphere? Look carefully. There are other shapes apart from hemispheres.

Igloos were often built like hemispheres.

A WORLD OF SPHERES

Of course, one of the most famous spheres is the one on which we live, the Earth. In fact, it is not a perfect sphere but slightly flattened at the North and South poles. This shape is called an **oblated sphere**. The other planets in our Solar System are spherical, too.

LINES AROUND THE GLOBE

On maps and globes, the Earth is often divided into two parts, the Northern and Southern Hemispheres. The division is made by an imaginary circle around the Earth, half way between the North and South Pole. This circle is called the Equator.

To help work out where we are on the Earth, mapmakers have created lots of imaginary lines around its spherical shape. They are called lines of latitude and longitude.

Latitude lines are parallel circles with their centre on the line joining the North and South poles. The Equator is a line of latitude.

Longitude lines are circles whose circumferences pass through both the North and South poles. This means they are at right angles to the lines of latitude.

Equator

Spherical shapes are very common in the natural world: many of the fruits we eat are spherical, and so are the grains of sand in a desert.

GLOSSARY

Annulus: the shape left when one circle is cut from the centre of another. It is like a washer.

 Anticlockwise: circular movement in the opposite direction to the turning of the hands of a clock.

Arc: part of the circumference of a circle.

Major arc: an arc that is bigger than a semicircle.

Minor arc: an arc that is smaller than a semicircle.

Axle: a rod in the centre of a circle or wheel around which it can turn or spin; also called a pivot.

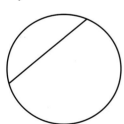 **Chord:** a straight line which crosses a circle from one point on its circumference to another, but does not pass through its centre.

Circumference: the curved edge of a circle which surrounds its centre, giving the distance all round it. The circumference of a circle is sometimes called its perimeter.

Clockwise: circular movement in the same direction as the hands of a clock.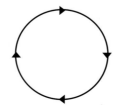

Concentric circles: different sized circles with the same centre.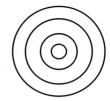

Curve: a line which has no straight part. Open curves have two ends, closed curves have no ends. A circle is a closed curve.

 Cylinder: a 3-D shape with two circular ends which are both the same size.

Diameter: a straight line which crosses a circle through its centre, connecting one point on its circumference with another.

 **Discs:** very thin cylinders, such as coins. Disc can also be spelt disk.

Ellipse: an oval shape like a slightly flattened circle.

Helix: a 3-D spiral shaped like a cylinder.

 Hemisphere: half of a sphere.

Latitude: the name given to imaginary parallel circles that surround the Earth from the North to South Poles. Along with lines of longitude, they are drawn on maps to indicate a position on the globe.

Longitude: the name given to imaginary circles whose

circumferences pass through both the North and South Poles and through lines of latitude at right angles.

Oblated sphere: a sphere which is slightly flattened at opposite ends.

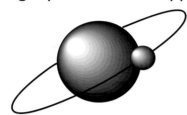

Orbit: the circular or elliptical path of an object moving around a sphere. The Moon is in orbit around the Earth and the Earth and other planets are in orbit around the Sun.

Oval: a closed curve that is either an egg shape or a slightly flattened circle shape which is sometimes called an ellipse.

Pivot: rod at the centre of a circle or wheel around which it can turn or spin; also called an axle.

Quadrant: a quarter section of a circle.

Radius: a straight line from the centre of a circle to the circumference. The length of a circle's radius is often used to express the circle's size, so a 4 cm circle has a radius of 4 cm. More than one radius are called radii.

Right angle: the angle formed by a quarter of a complete turn. A right angle is sometimes called a square corner. The angle where the two straight lines of quadrant meet is a right angle.

Sector: a slice of a circle made by cutting along two radii.

Major sector: a sector that is bigger than a semicircle.

Minor sector: a sector that is smaller than a semicircle.

Segment: a slice of a circle made by cutting along a chord. When a circle is cut into two segments, the larger segment is called the major segment and the smaller one the minor segment.

Semicircle: half a circle.

Sphere: a 3-D shape that has no flat surfaces and no corners. A sphere is a perfectly round ball. Every point on a sphere's surface is exactly the same distance from its centre as every other point.

Spherical: describes something that looks like a sphere.

Spiral: a coil; a curve growing from the centre of a circle. A spiral can be 2-D or 3-D.

Torus: a 3-D shape like a doughnut or inner tube that has no flat surfaces.

INDEX